MAKE AND PLAY

HATS GALORE

W. G. Alton

Mills & Boon Limited
London Toronto Sydney

Owlet books are published by Mills & Boon Limited.
First published in Great Britain 1975 by Mills & Boon
Limited, 17–19 Foley Street, London W1A 1DR.

ISBN 0 263.05936.7

Made and Printed by C. Nicholls & Company Ltd, The Philips Park Press,
Manchester M11 4AU

Contents

Introduction

These hats can be made for plays or parties, or just because you want to make a hat — which is a very good reason indeed.

You should make some simple hats first before trying to make the more difficult ones. When you have selected a hat to make, it is a good idea to read through the instructions first and see that you have the necessary materials.

When a hat has a soft floppy crown, the crown can be made from crêpe paper or tissue paper, but thin metallized plastic foil, or aluminium foil, will look more attractive. Plain or coloured cardboard headbands, and other cardboard parts, can be covered with patterned paper, metallic paper or metal foil paper.

I am sure you will enjoy making and wearing paper hats. You can make up your own designs for other hats using different papers and colours.

Materials you will need

Cardboard: coloured and plain.

Paper: tissue, crêpe and patterned paper. Although not essential, thin metallized plastic foil, aluminium foil, metal foil paper and metallized paper will make the hats extremely attractive for party wear.

Sticky tape: this is easier to use if it is in a dispenser, but the dispenser is not essential.

Gummed paper tape: use for making firm crown shapes, as for the King Lear helmet.

Sheets of newspaper: spread these out over the working surface to catch any waste materials.

Glue: P.V.A. or Seccotine were used for the hats in this book, but other glues suitable for gluing cardboard will do.

Scissors.

Clothes pegs: these are useful for holding pieces of cardboard together while the glue dries.

Ruler: about 30cm long.

Pencil, paints and crayons.

A pair of compasses.

Stapler: useful, but not essential.

Beret

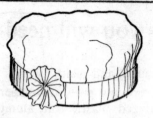

1. To make the headband, cut a strip of medium-thickness coloured cardboard about 65cm x 3cm.

2. Wrap this round your head, not too tightly, and hold it between finger and thumb as a ring. Mark the extent of the overlap with a pencil.

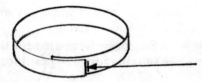

3. Glue the overlap and cover the ends of the headband with sticky tape, or hold with clothes pegs to keep the join in place while the glue dries.

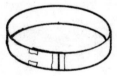 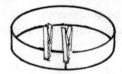

4. Cut a square of tissue paper, about 40cm x 40cm, for the crown of the hat. Crêpe or other thin paper can be used instead.

5. Fold lightly into quarters and cut the corners with scissors, so that when opened the paper will be circular.

6 Using a length of sticky tape, about 3cm long, fix the paper crown to the inside of the headband.

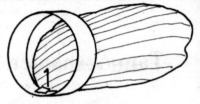

7 Turn headband round and sticky-tape the opposite side.

8 Sticky-tape two more opposite places.

9 Now sticky-tape four more places between the first four, then continue all round until the crown is firmly held in place.

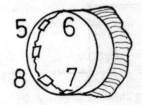

10 To make a rosette, cut a piece of paper about 50cm x 7cm. Pleat the paper, then screw up one end and insert it in a pierced hole in the front of the headband. Secure twisted end with a piece of sticky tape, about 3cm long.

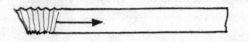

Tam-o'-shanter

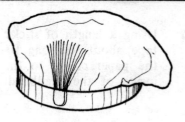

1   Make the headband as for the Beret on page 6. Cut a square of tissue paper, 55cm x 55cm, for the crown. Attach the crown to the headband as for the Beret on page 6 (steps 5, 6, 7, 8 and 9).

2   To make a plume, cut a piece of thin cardboard, about 10cm x 15cm, and glue some attractive paper (metallized paper would be ideal) to both sides. Now make some long cuts, about 3mm or 4mm apart, and stopping about 3cm from one edge. Fold or roll the cardboard and place plume inside or outside the headband. Glue and sticky-tape, or staple, plume to headband.

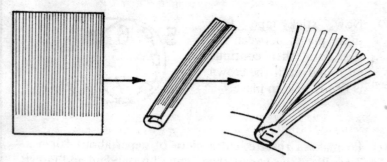

A useful way of having a ready supply of sticky-tape is to cut some to the required length and lightly stick these lengths to the edge of a table until they are required.

Chef's hat

1   Make the headband from white cardboard as for the Beret on page 6.

2   Make the crown from a piece of white crêpe or tissue paper, about 60cm x 35cm. Join the two short edges with sticky tape.

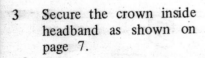

3   Secure the crown inside headband as shown on page 7.

4   Gather in the top edges, pinching them into a point at the centre. Sticky-tape the edges together on the inside.

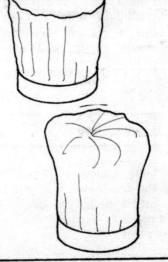

Crown 1

1   Cut a strip of cardboard about 65cm x 6cm. Wrap it round your head and mark the overlap with a pencil as shown on page 6.

2   Divide the length of the headband into eight equal parts. This can be done by cutting a strip of paper to this length and folding it in half three times. Lay paper against headband and mark off folds.

3   Fold a small piece of thin cardboard in half and cut out a pattern for the curves on the headband.

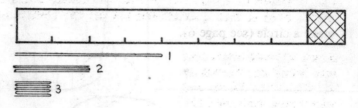

4   Put your pattern on the headband and pencil in the curves.

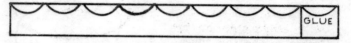

5   Glue a piece of metallized paper to the other side of the headband. Cut out the curves. Glue the headband into a circle.

6 Make the top from a circle of tissue paper, or metallized plastic foil, about 45cm across, and sticky-tape it into the headband as shown on page 7.

7 Cut a strip of cardboard, about 30cm x 4cm. Turn crown upside down, then sticky-tape strip to inside of headband. (The diagram shows the hat without its top.)

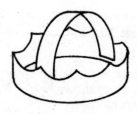

8 Cut a square of metallized plastic foil, about 20cm x 20cm. Fold it into quarters and cut off the corners to make a circle (see page 6).

9 Screw up some newspaper into a ball and wrap it up in the foil. Twist and sticky-tape the loose ends.

10 Pierce a hole through the centre of cardboard strip and the plastic foil covering it. Push the twisted end of the ball through the holes and secure it with sticky tape on the inside.

Crown 2

1 Make the headband from cardboard as for Crown 1 on page 10.

2 Mark and cut out four pieces of cardboard for the cross-bands as shown below. Cover these pieces with metallized paper.

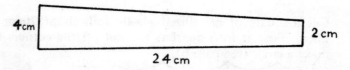

4cm   2 cm
                        24 cm

3 Glue and sticky-tape them into the headband. Clothes pegs can be used to keep them in place.

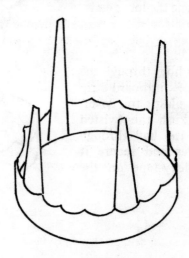

4   Cut a circle of metallized foil or tissue paper, about 50cm across, as shown on page 6 (steps 4 and 5). Now sticky-tape this into the headband (see page 7).

5   Bend and shape the crossbands so that they overlap in the centre by about 3cm. Glue and sticky-tape cross-bands together.

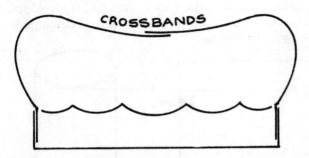

CROSSBANDS

6   Make rosettes from metallized plastic foil or tissue paper, as shown on page 7. Insert them round the headband.

7   Draw a cross on cardboard and leave a 2cm square gluing flap at the lower edge. Use coins for drawing the circles. Cut out cross and glue it to a second piece of cardboard, leaving second flap unglued as shown. Cover with metallized paper. Cut to shape. Glue and sticky-tape cross to top of crown.

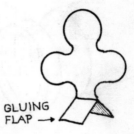

GLUING FLAP →

13

One-piece hat

1   Make the headband from cardboard as for the Beret on page 6.

2   The crown is made in one piece. Cut a piece of metallized plastic foil, or crêpe paper, about 65cm x 45cm, and make this into a tube (cylinder) using sticky tape to join the two short edges.

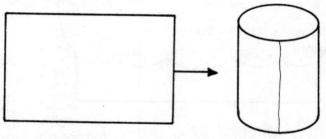

3   Slip the headband inside the crown and sticky-tape the edges of the crown to the headband as shown.

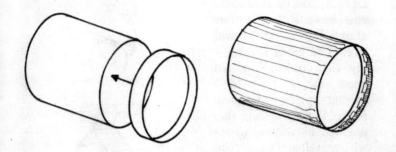

4 Pull the crown through the headband as shown.

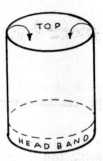

5 Fringe the top edge of the crown.

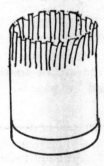

6 Gather the fringe together and tie, or use a small elastic band.

Forage cap

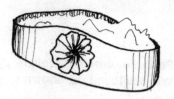

1 Make the headband to fit the head, as shown on page 6.

2 Cut out a circular crown, 35 cm across, as shown on page 6. Sticky-tape this crown to the outside of the headband. Follow the general instructions for fixing the crown to the headband on page 7.

3 Cut a piece of cardboard to the same length as the headband and about 10 cm wide. Glue metallized paper to one side.

4 Wrap the cardboard strip round the headband and mark the overlap with a pencil.

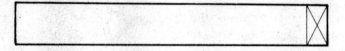

5 Divide this cardboard strip into four equal parts, as shown below.

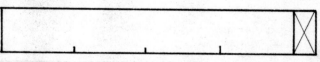

6 Make a quarter pattern as shown in the shaded diagram below.

Draw round this pattern with a pencil on to the cardboard strip, to make the complete curved edge as shown. Cut to this line.

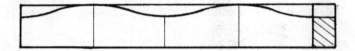

7 Glue this curved strip of cardboard round the outer headband. Use clothes pegs as you go to hold it in place until the glue has dried.

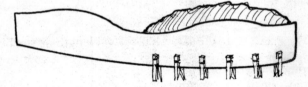

8 Cut out two circles of metallized foil, about 12cm across, and make these two layers into a rosette by twisting the centres. Insert this rosette in a hole through the headband.

Yachtsman's cap

1   Make the headband as shown on page 6. This can be made from coloured cardboard, or plain cardboard covered with attractive paper.

2   Make a circular crown from metallized paper, crêpe paper or tissue paper, about 35cm across. Sticky-tape the crown to the inside of headband as shown on page 7.

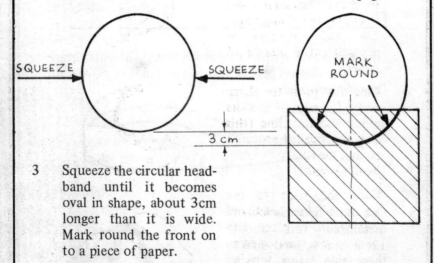

SQUEEZE →   ← SQUEEZE

MARK ROUND

3 cm

3   Squeeze the circular headband until it becomes oval in shape, about 3cm longer than it is wide. Mark round the front on to a piece of paper.

4   Sketch in half the peak and some gluing flaps round the inside of the peak, so that it can be fixed to the headband at a later stage.

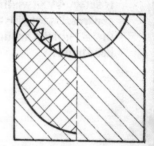

5 Now fold the paper in half on the centre line as shown and cut round both halves when they are pressed together. When the paper is opened out, you will have a nicely shaped pattern.

Now use this to mark round, with a pencil, on to a piece of cardboard, or glue the pattern to a piece of cardboard. Cut to shape. Remember not to cut off the gluing flaps! The peak can now be covered with metallized paper.

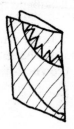

6 Carefully press the sharp end of a pair of scissors along the flap line (this process is called scoring), so that the flaps will easily bend upright.

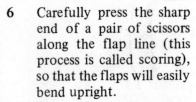

7 Glue the flaps to the inside of the headband and secure in place with sticky tape, starting from the middle and working outwards in both directions. Press down firmly on the edge of a table as shown.

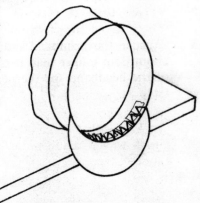

Jockey cap

1   Make the headband as shown on page 6.

2   For the crown, cut out a circle of metallized plastic foil, crêpe or tissue paper, about 35cm across. Sticky-tape this crown to the inside of the headband as shown on page 7.

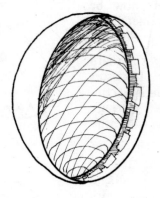

3   Squeeze the headband until it becomes oval in shape, about 3cm longer than it is wide. Mark round the front of the headband for the peak line, as shown on page 18 (step 3).

4 Mark out and make the peak as shown on pages 18 and 19.

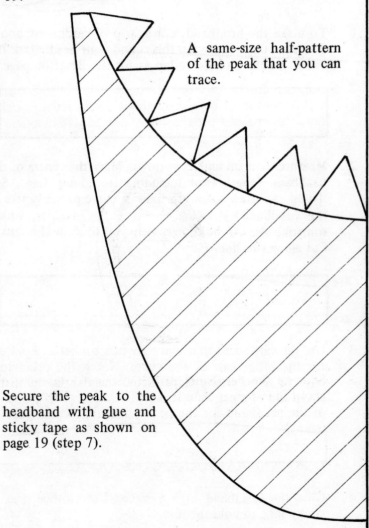

A same-size half-pattern of the peak that you can trace.

5 Secure the peak to the headband with glue and sticky tape as shown on page 19 (step 7).

Guardsman's cap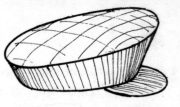

1   To make the headband, cut a strip of cardboard, about 65cm x 10cm, and wrap this round your head. Mark the extent of the gluing overlap as for the Beret on page 6.

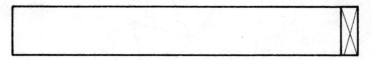

2   Measure 2cm up and 2cm down. Mark the centre of the headband length (not including the gluing flap). See if you can draw a smooth shallow curve to the centre of the headband. Drawing round a flexed ruler, which someone else can hold, may help you to draw this curve. Cut along this line.

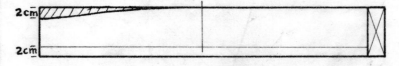

3   Use the cardboard that you have just cut off as a pattern for the other half of the curve. Notch the other long edge to form gluing flaps. Score the flap line with the sharp end of a pair of scissors.

4   Glue the headband into a circle. Use clothes pegs or sticky tape to hold the join.

5   Cut out a piece of thin cardboard, or very thick paper, about 27cm x 24cm, and fold it in half twice.

6   Now draw a smooth curve as shown, so that when you open out the cardboard it will be an ellipse (oval). Cut out this pattern.

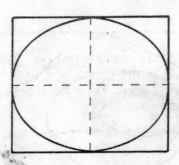

7   Draw round this pattern for the crown on thick cardboard and then cut it out.

8 Glue the headband to the crown. The gluing flaps can be held down with sticky tape. The headband should be positioned about 3cm in from one end of the crown as shown. The headband should be squeezed a little so that it is about 3cm longer than it is wide, as shown on page 18 (step 3).

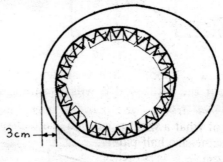

9 Place the cap upside down on a piece of metallized plastic foil, or crêpe paper, and cut the foil so that there is enough to cover the crown, the sides and to fold inside the headband.

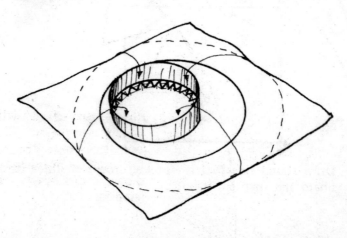

10 Sticky-tape the foil to the inside of the headband.

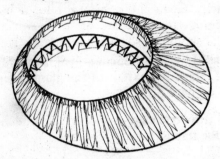

11 Now make a peak using the method shown on pages 18 and 19. The drawing at the top of page 22 will give you an idea of what a short peak on a guardsman's cap looks like. A same-size half-pattern of the peak is shown below.

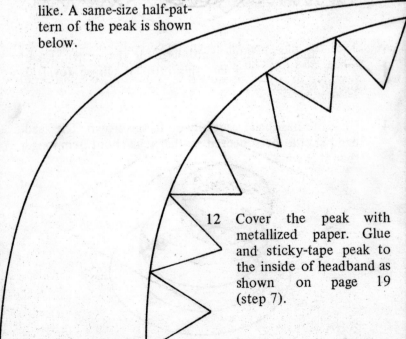

12 Cover the peak with metallized paper. Glue and sticky-tape peak to the inside of headband as shown on page 19 (step 7).

Bandsman's cap

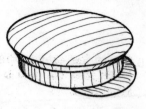

1 Cut a cardboard headband, about 65 cm x 9 cm, and wrap it round your head. Mark the extent of the gluing overlap as for the Beret on page 6.

2 Draw a line 2 cm up from one edge as shown, and cut the gluing flaps. Score the flap line.

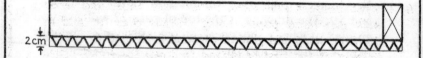

2 cm

3 Cut a piece of thick cardboard for the crown, about 27 cm x 24 cm, and cut this into an ellipse (oval) as shown on page 23.

4 Glue the headband centrally on to the crown. The headband should be squeezed so that it is about 3 cm longer than it is wide.

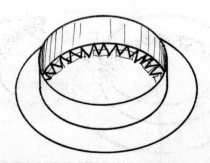

5   Cover the crown with metallized plastic foil or paper. Note that the foil is sticky-taped to the outside of the headband.

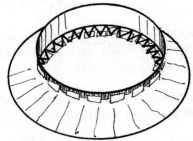

6   Make another headband, about 4cm wide, and cover with metallized paper. Using clothes pegs to hold in position, wrap and glue this second headband round the outside of the first headband to cover the rough edges of the foil and securing sticky tape.

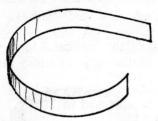

7   Make a peak to fit cap as shown on pages 18 and 19.

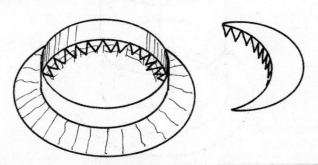

French hat

1   Cut a cardboard headband, about 65cm x 12cm, and wrap it round your head. Mark the extent of the gluing overlap as for the Beret on page 6.

2   Draw a line 2cm up from one edge as shown, and cut the gluing flaps. Score the flap line.

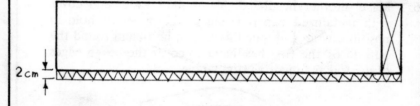

3   Glue the ends of the headband together. Hold the join in place with clothes pegs or sticky tape.

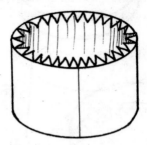

4 To mark out the crown, lightly sticky-tape the headband to a piece of cardboard (shaded in diagram below), so that the headband is oval in shape, as shown on page 18. Draw round the crown with a pencil. Remove the sticky tape and cut out the oval crown. Now glue the flaps and fix the crown to the headband. Sticky tape will help to hold the gluing flaps in place.

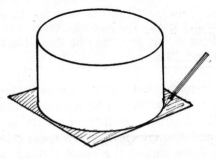

5 The hat can now be covered with paper or foil.

6 Cut out the peak from cardboard and cover with metallized paper. Glue the flaps and sticky-tape these in position inside the hat as shown on pages 18 and 19.

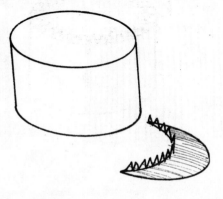

Fez

1   Cut a cardboard headband, about 65cm x 12cm. Wrap this round your head and test for fit, leaving an overlap for joining as shown on page 28.

2   To make and cover the crown, follow the instructions for the French hat (leaving out those for the peak) on pages 28 and 29.

3   Make a tassel by cutting a piece of metallized plastic foil, which is attractive on both sides, or glue two pieces of metallized paper together. A length of fancy string can be glued into the tassel as it is being rolled and glued together. Then thread the tassel through a hole in the top of the crown and secure with sticky tape.

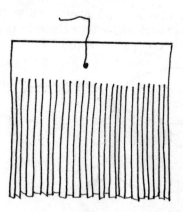
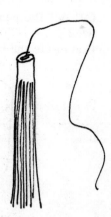

Bonnet

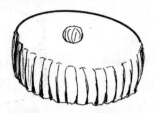

1   Cut a cardboard headband, about 65cm x 12cm. Wrap this round your head and test for fit, leaving an overlap for joining as shown on page 28.

2   To make the crown, follow the instructions for the French hat (leaving out those for the peak) on pages 28 and 29.

3   Cover with metallized plastic foil or crêpe paper.

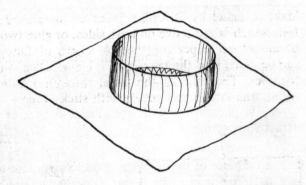

4   Sticky-tape the plastic foil covering inside the hat.

5   Finish the hat with a ball as shown on page 11.

Straw hat

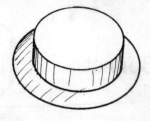

1   Cut a cardboard headband, about 65cm x 11cm. Wrap this round your head and test for fit, leaving an overlap for gluing. Cut the gluing flaps and glue the ends of headband together, as shown on page 28 (steps 2 and 3).

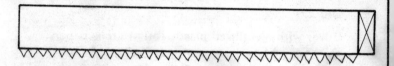

2   Now cut out the crown from cardboard. Glue and sticky-tape this to the headband as shown on page 29.

3   Cover the headband with metallized paper, or other attractive covering.

4   Cut out a piece of paper to cover the crown. Use the hat as a pattern for marking it out. Glue it over the crown.

5   Now get a sheet of fairly thick cardboard and set the hat on it, leaving a margin of about 5cm all round the hat for the brim.
    Mark round the hat with a pencil.

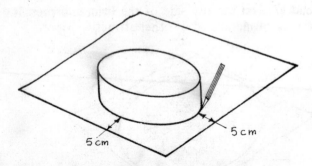

5 cm

5 cm

6   Remove the hat and set a pair of compasses to 5cm.
     With the point of the compasses on the oval, draw a
     curve and repeat this about ten times as shown. Sketch
     in the outer curve of the brim. Cut to this line.

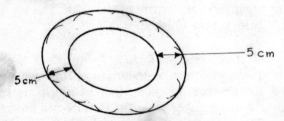

5 cm

5cm

7   Mark in the gluing flaps 2cm inside, and score the flap
     line. Pierce a hole in the middle of this piece of card-
     board and gradually cut the brim to the shape as shown.

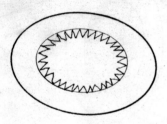

8   Spread glue on the top side of the brim and press it on to a piece of metallized or other attractive paper.

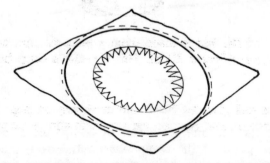

9   Cut off the spare paper, leaving about 1 cm all round (dotted line) to turn over and glue down. Cut out the spare paper from the centre of the brim. The top surface of the brim is now finished.

10 Glue and sticky-tape the flaps to the inside of the crown. Now spread glue on the underside of the brim and press it on to the covering paper that you have chosen. Cut away the spare paper from the outside and inside of the brim. The hat can be finished with a hatband of ribbon, or a strip of paper.

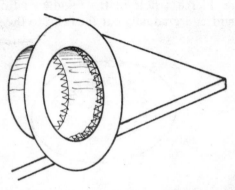

High hat

1   The side of the hat is made from a piece of thin cardboard, about 65cm x 20cm. This is really a deep headband.

2   Mark out and glue the headband as shown on page 28. Also mark out and glue on the crown as shown on page 29.

3   Cut out a piece of paper to cover the headband. This can be glued on, but if crêpe or tissue paper is used, then it should be sticky-taped inside and on top of the crown.

4   Cut out and glue on a covering for the crown.

5   Make a small peak as shown on pages 18 and 19.

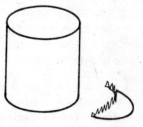

Witch's hat

1   Cut, make and glue a headband, about 65cm x 3cm, as shown on page 6.

2   To make the brim, squeeze the headband so that it is 3cm longer than it is wide, as shown on page 18. Set this shape with sticky tape on to a piece of cardboard. Allow for a brim of 6cm.

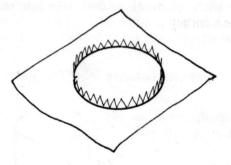

3   Using a ruler or a pair of compasses, mark 6cm about ten times from the flap line. Sketch in the brim and cut it out as shown on page 33.

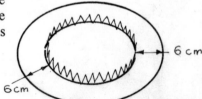

4   Cut a strip of cardboard, about 30cm x 3cm, to form a 'compass arm'. The compass will pivot on a drawing pin as shown below.

PENCIL

DRAWING PIN

5   Get a piece of thin cardboard and use the cardboard compass to draw the broken line as shown below. Use a tape measure to measure the distance round the gluing flaps of the brim. Add about 5cm to this measurement and, again, use the tape measure to mark off this length along the curve (broken line on diagram). Draw the two straight lines marked 'A' to form the shaded shape of the pointed crown. Cut out this shaded shape and roll it into a cone, like a cornet.

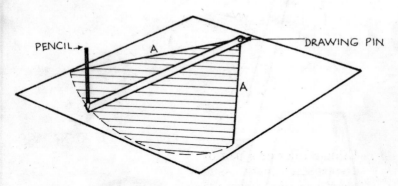

PENCIL

DRAWING PIN

A

A

6   When gluing the pointed crown (cone) to the brim, start at the centre of the curved edge and sticky-tape in position. Work to the left and right and finish by gluing and sticky-taping the long straight edges of the pointed crown. Work on the edge of a table as shown on page 34. The hat can be decorated with metallized paper stars and moon.

Guy Fawkes' hat

1   Make a brim as shown on page 36 (steps 1, 2 and 3).

2   Sketch a full-size side view of the hat as shown. Remember that you should start with the brim size, which you have already made. Now draw in the two broken lines as shown. You now have two measurements, shown by the arrowed lines 'A' and 'B'.

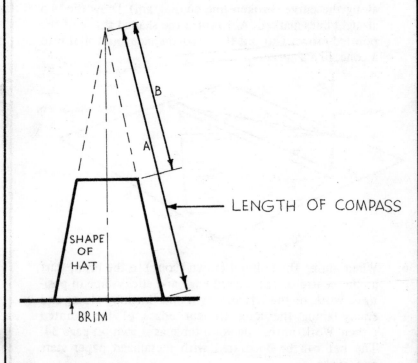

LENGTH OF COMPASS

SHAPE OF HAT

BRIM

3   Make a cardboard compass as shown on page 37, with 'A' as the length of the compass. Now draw the curve 'a' on a piece of thin cardboard and also the curve 'b'. (If the drawing pin is off the cardboard, then a piece of cardboard can be sticky-taped on the table as shown below.) Read carefully through the instructions for making the crown of the Witch's hat and finish drawing the shape shaded in the diagram below.

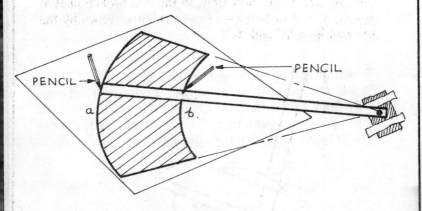

4   Add 2cm gluing flaps as shown.

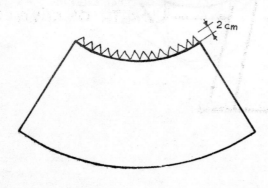

5   Glue and sticky-tape this crown into the brim as shown below.

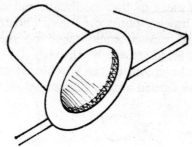

6   Turn the hat upside down on to a piece of cardboard. Steady the hat with a weight (not too heavy!) and carefully draw round the top. Remove the hat. Cut out the top. Glue and sticky-tape the top to hat. A feather — real or paper — will improve the appearance.

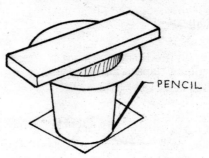

PENCIL

Coolie hat

1   Use a pair of compasses set to 18cm radius and draw a circle on a piece of cardboard. Cut out this circle.

2   Draw a line from the circle to its centre and cut along this line.

3   This cut will allow a cone (like a cornet) to be formed by overlapping the two edges. An overlap of about 10cm at the edge of the circle will form a good shape. This overlap can now be glued and held in place with clothes pegs.

4   Cut two lengths of ribbon about 30cm long. Pass these through two discs of cardboard, about 4cm across, and glue the ends of the ribbons to the discs. Now glue these inside the hat, leaving the ribbons hanging down to tie under the chin.

Cocked hat

1　Make the headband from cardboard, about 65cm x 3cm, as shown on page 6.

2　Draw a circle with a pair of compasses on a piece of paper. The circle should be the same size as the headband and a little experimentation may be necessary to find this size, but great accuracy is not essential. By keeping your compass set to the same measurement as you used for the circle, it is an easy matter to make the pattern as shown. This pattern will divide the circle into six equal parts. Place the headband on this circle and mark the six positions on the headband.

3　Cut three strips of cardboard, 30cm x 3cm. Glue the strips in position as shown. Try on the hat for fit as this is being done. Use sticky tape and clothes pegs to hold in place.

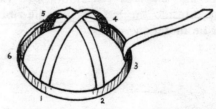

4 Cover with metallized plastic foil, crêpe paper or tissue paper as shown on page 31.

5 For the brim cut out a circle about 40cm across.

6 Squeeze the headband of the hat slightly so that it is about 3cm longer than it is wide, as shown on page 18. Place the crown on the centre of the 40cm circle for the brim and draw round the crown on to the circle. Draw in the 2cm gluing flaps. Cut out the brim.

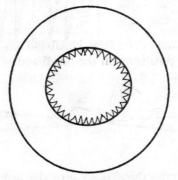

7 Cover the brim with metallized paper and glue the crown to the brim as shown on page 34. Roll up the edges of the brim, pierce holes through the three crossbands and the brim, and secure with paper twists as shown on page 11. Glue and sticky-tape these to the inside of the crossbands.

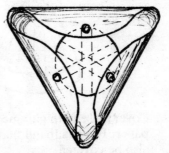

King Lear helmet

1   Make a headband from cardboard, about 65cm x 4cm, as shown on page 6.

2   Cut a sheet of cardboard 30cm x 20cm. Mark 3cm intervals all along the two long edges and join with lines as shown. Cut out these triangles.

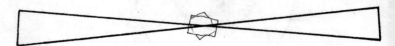

3   Join these triangles in pairs with sticky tape.

4   Glue and sticky-tape these pairs into the headband, on opposite sides, so that the points of the triangles form the point of the helmet.

5   Cover these with gummed paper. The headband may also be covered.

6   Spray or paint the helmet silver.

7   Cut out another headband, 5cm wide and the same length as the first headband. Cover it with silver metallized paper. Glue this, using clothes pegs to secure, to the outside of the first headband.

8   The emblems shown on the finished helmet are traced on to cardboard, using the same-size pattern below. Cover the emblems with silver paper. Glue them to the outer headband, using clothes pegs to secure in place.

Schoolmaster's hat

1   Cut a piece of paper about 30cm x 26cm.

2   Fold it in half twice and cut off the corners to make an ellipse (oval) as shown on page 23. Use this as a pattern and cut out the shape in thin cardboard.

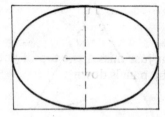

3   Repeat this with another piece of paper, about 14cm x 11cm. Use this to mark the second ellipse for the top of the crown.

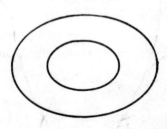

4   Draw some lines, about 3cm apart, all round the edge to the edge of the crown. Cut on these lines.

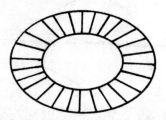

5   Bend these panels down and you will see that they overlap. Start to sticky-tape some of these panels down, overlapping by about 1cm at the edge. Keep testing for fit, until the crown just misses the top of your head. Finish sticky-taping the panels down.

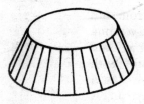

6   Bind the edges and the rest of the hat with gummed paper tape, or strips of paper glued on.

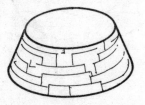

7 Use scissors to shape the front of the hat as shown.

8 For the top of the hat cut a piece of thick cardboard about 26cm x 26cm.

9 Glue the top of the crown to the square of cardboard. A weight inside will help to keep the two surfaces together. Spray or paint the whole hat black.

10 Make a tassel from old bits of string. Add a string and knot each time, then seal the large knot with glue. Secure the tassel into the hat by passing it through a hole in the crown. Glue the end inside the hat and hold in place with sticky tape.

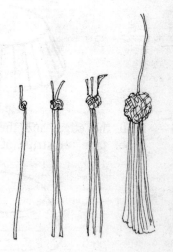